Teacup Trudy's
ABCs & 123s

A B C

1 2 3

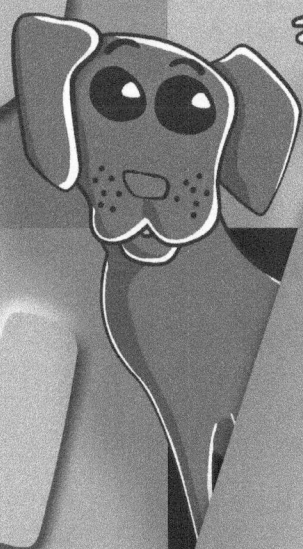

created by
Ron Pittman

Teacup Trudy's ABC's & 123's Coloring Book • © 2016 Ron Pittman

Printed in the United States States of America

Special thanks to Denise Oldham
Graphic Production by Springer Design & Illustration

Published by The Tender Times • Eugene, Oregon

ISBN: 978-0-692-78992-6

Your Name: _____

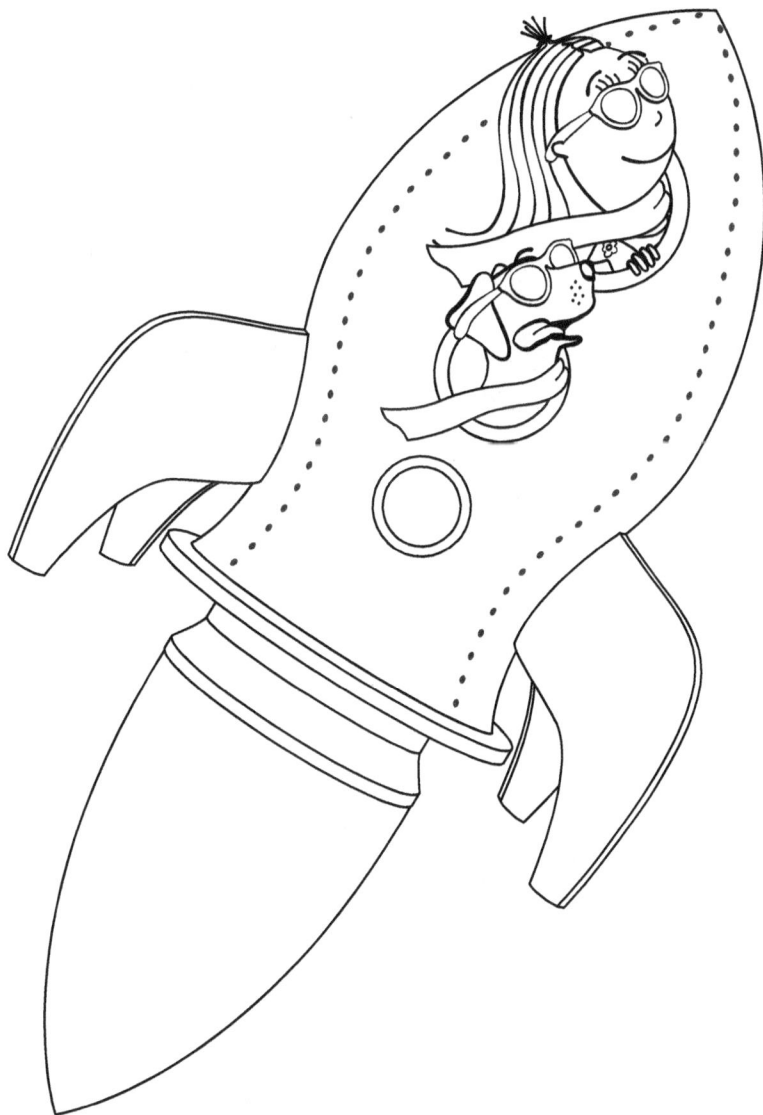

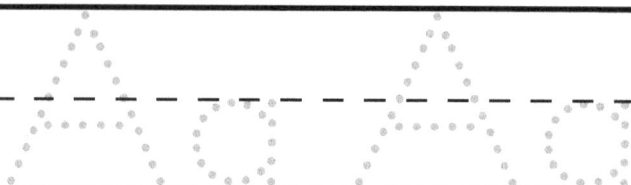

A a

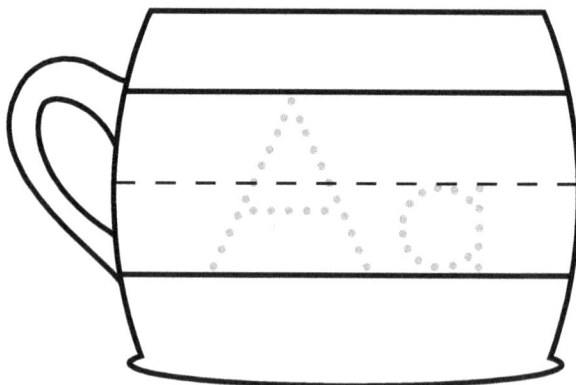

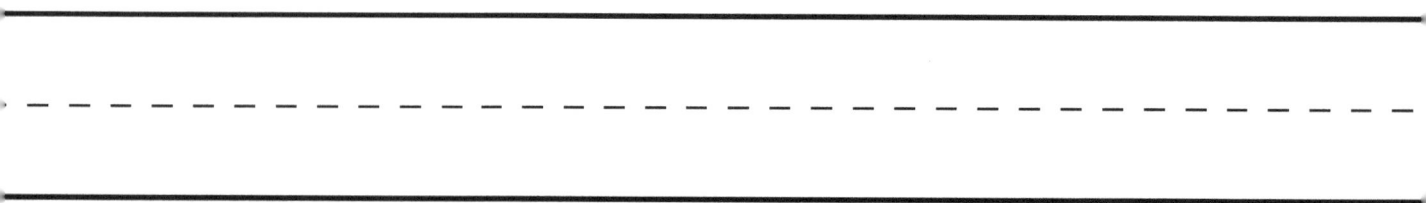

Bb Bb Bb

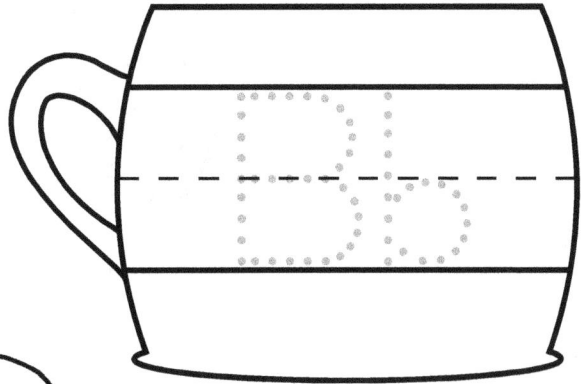

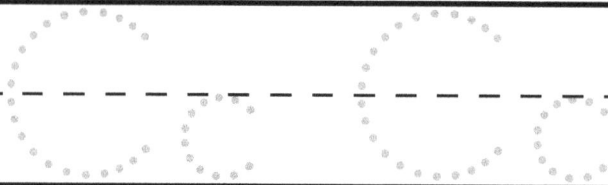

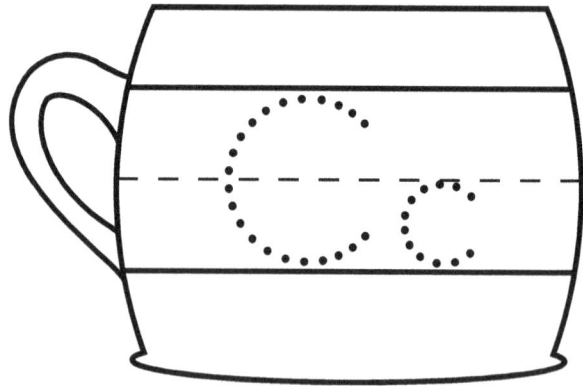

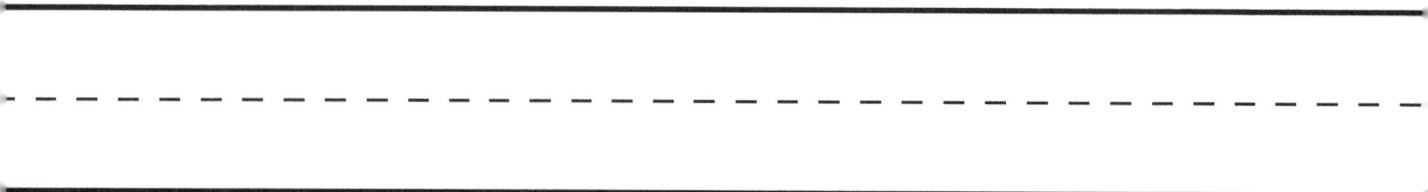

Dd

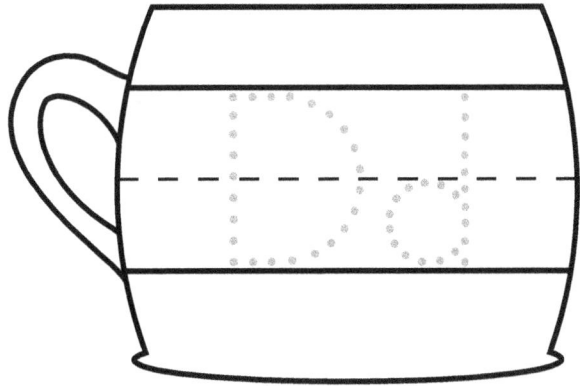

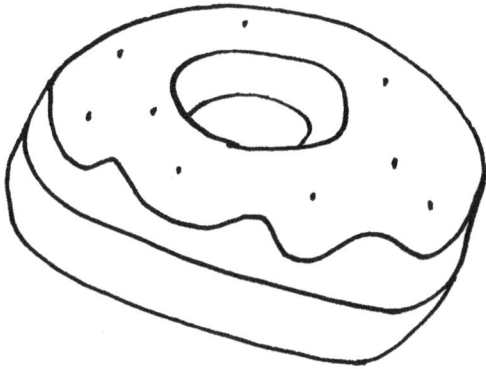

E e

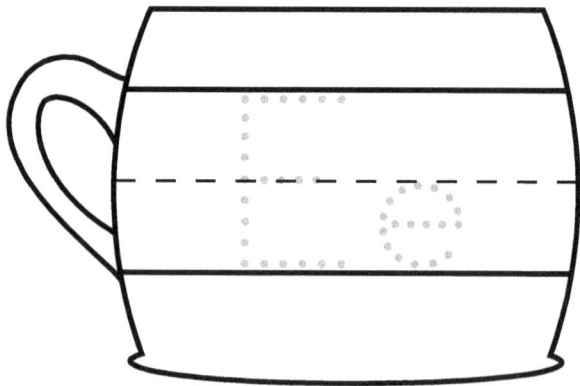

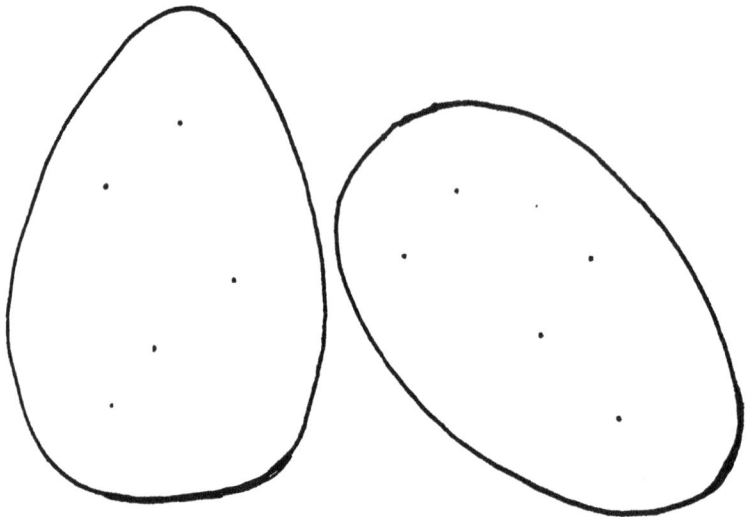

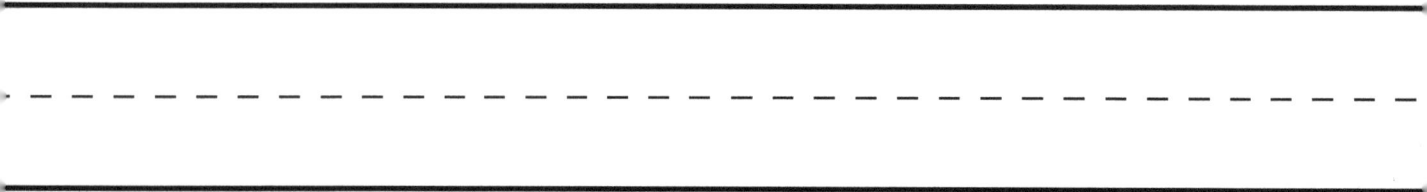

F f

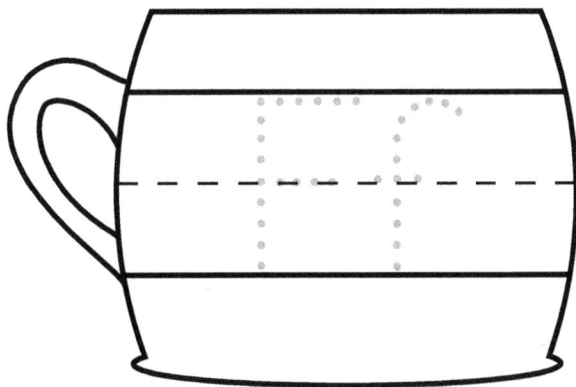

Gg

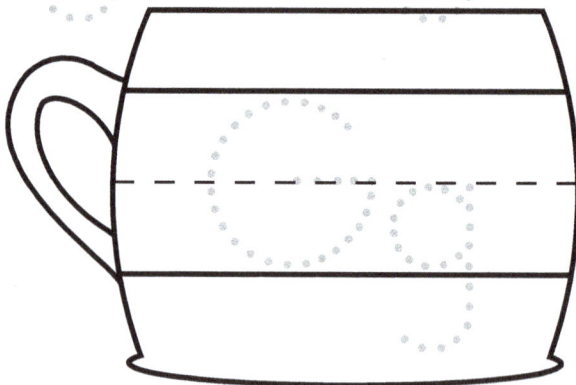

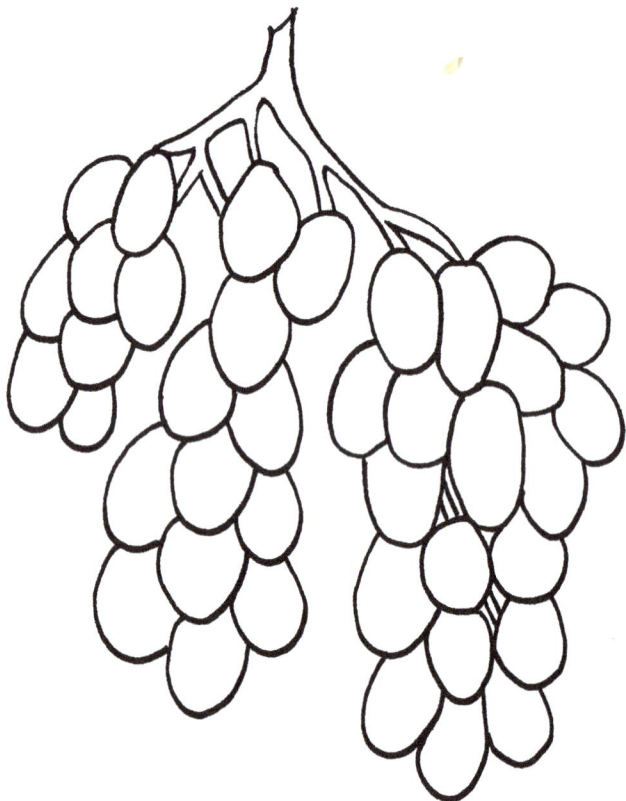

Hh

h h

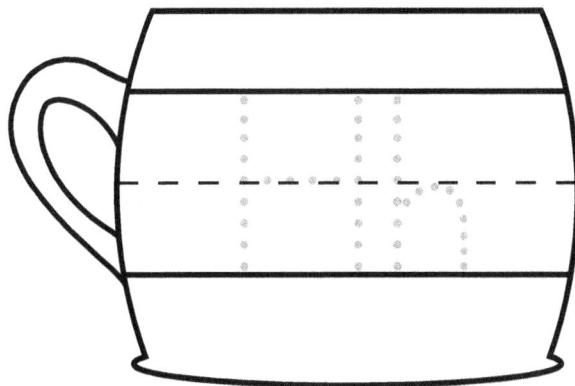

I i

J j

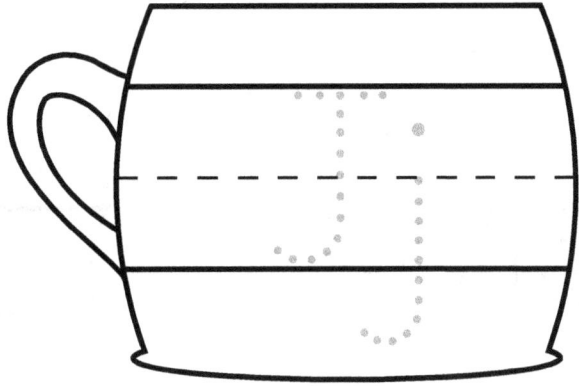

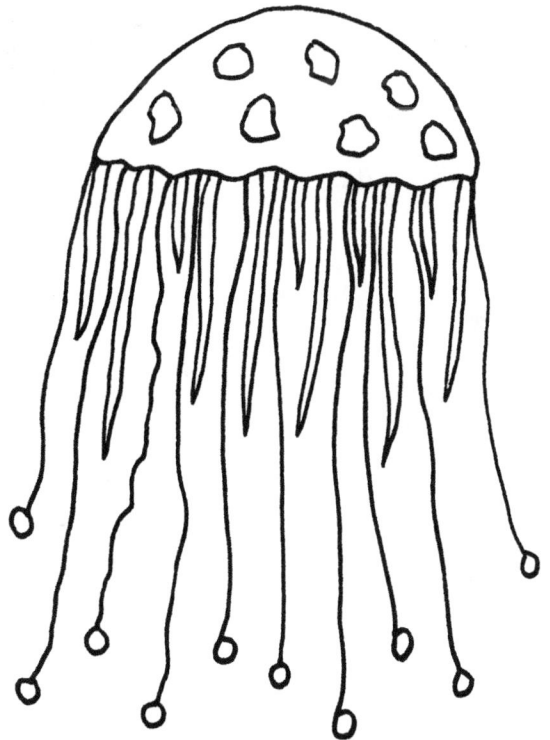

K k

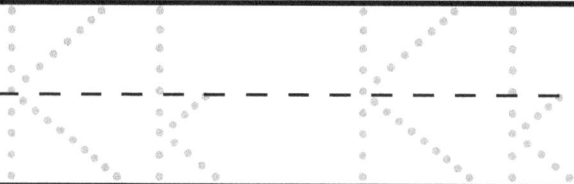

L

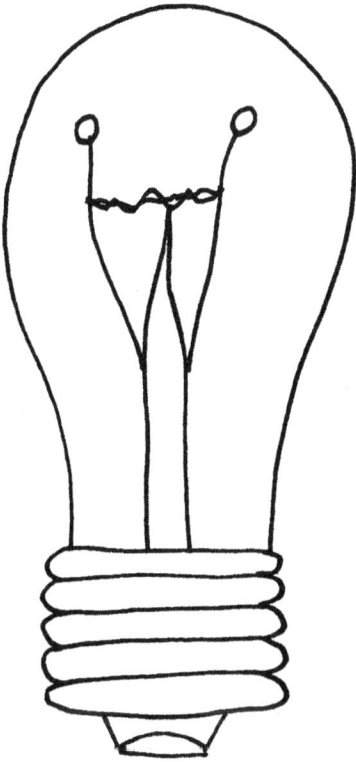

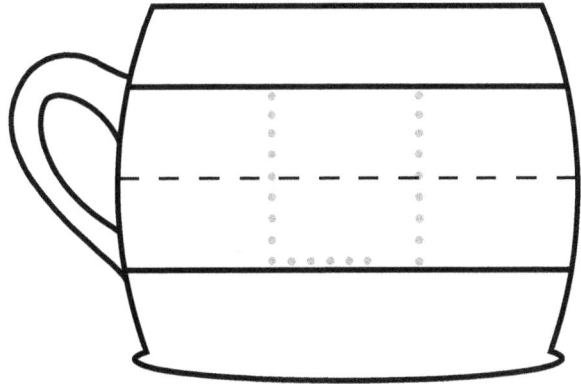

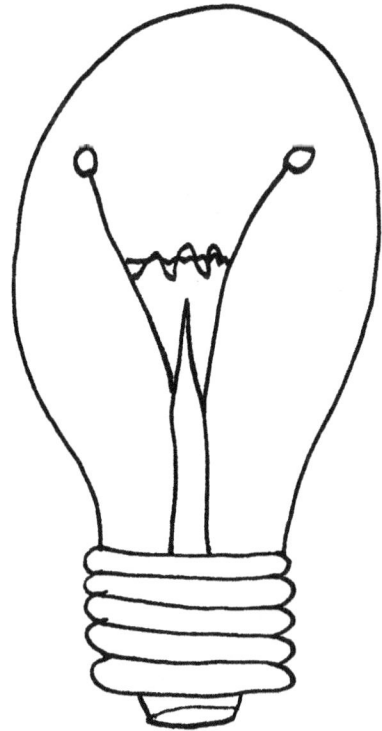

Mm

Mm Mm Mm

Mm

Nn

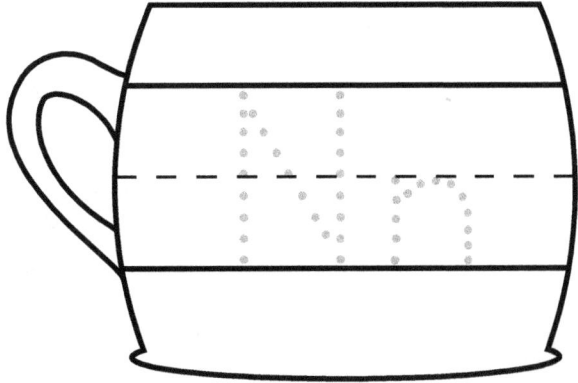

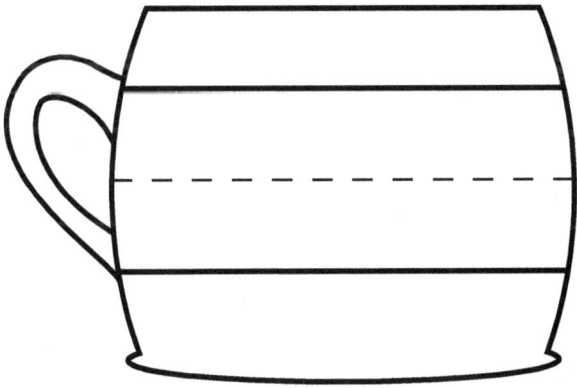

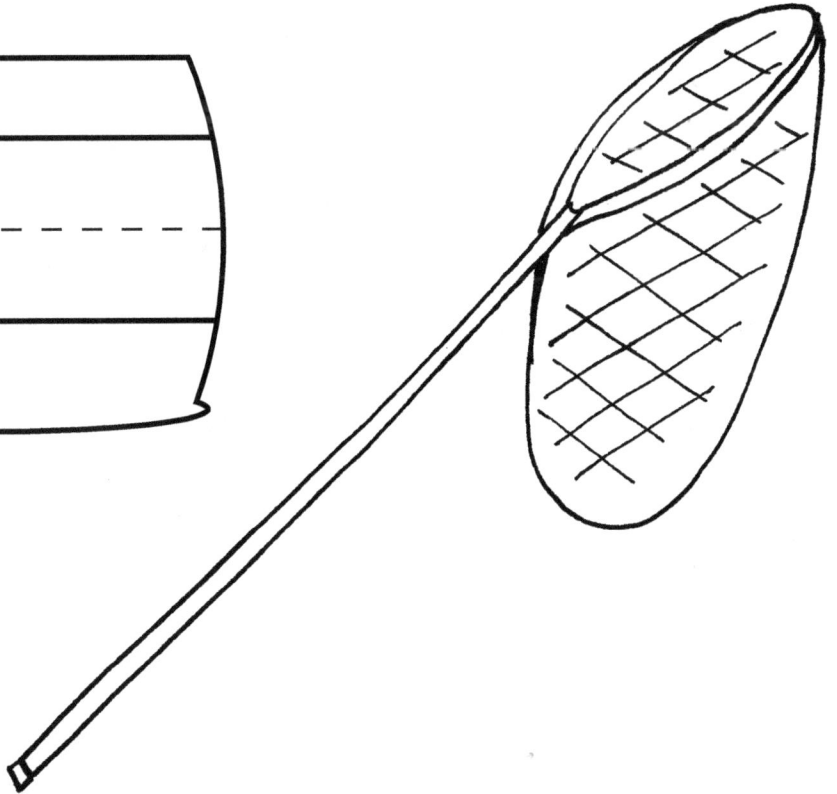

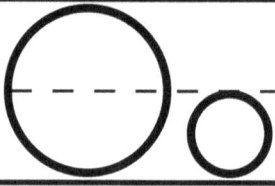

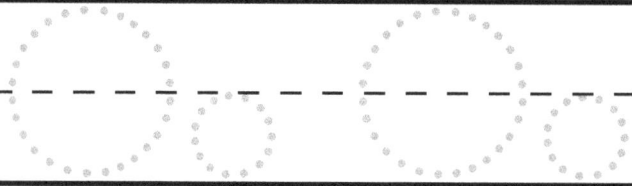

P p

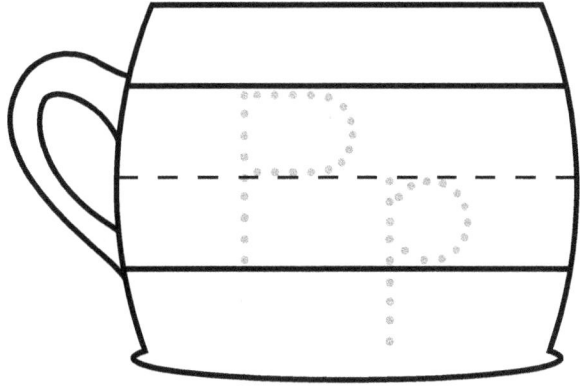

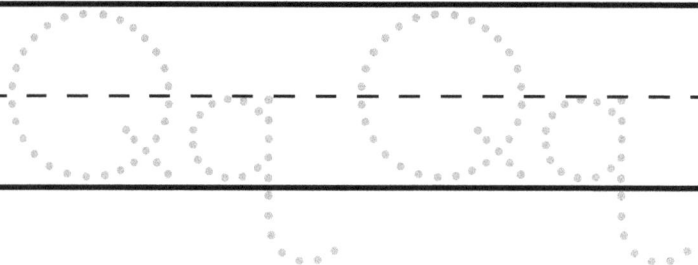

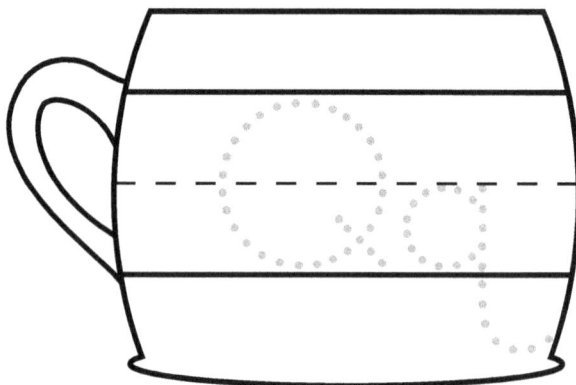

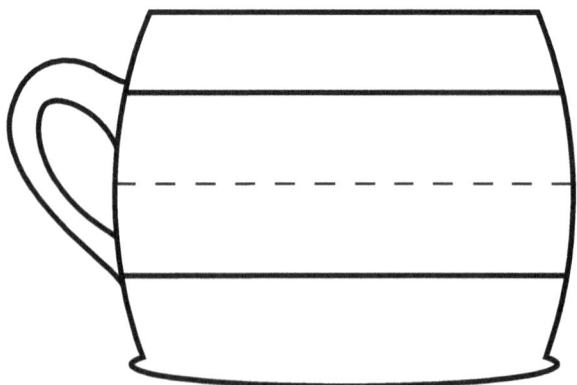

Rr

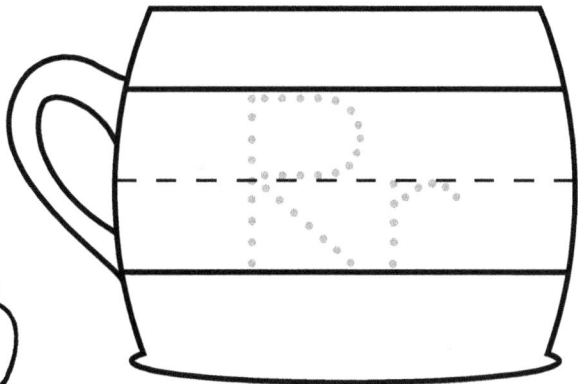

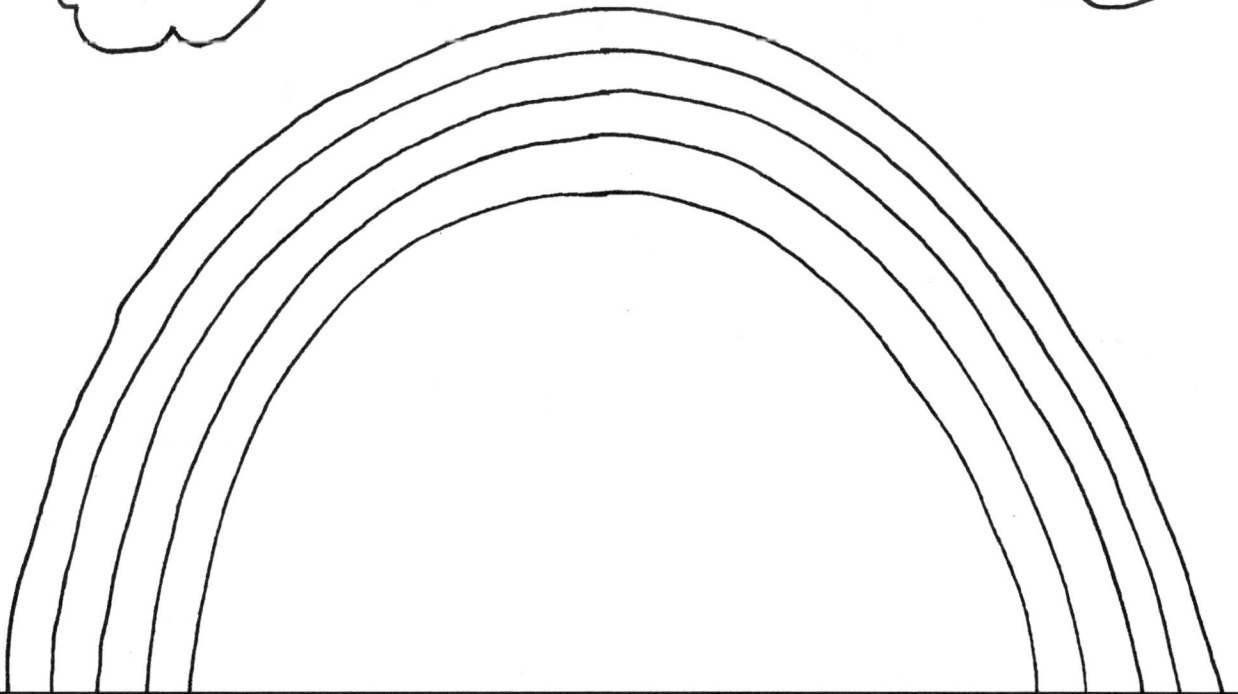

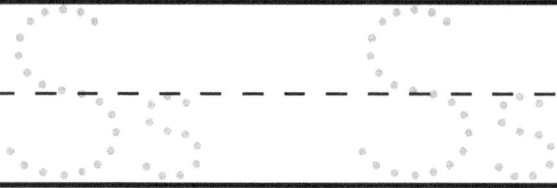

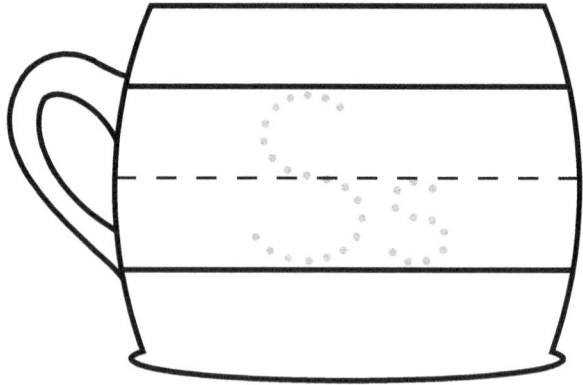

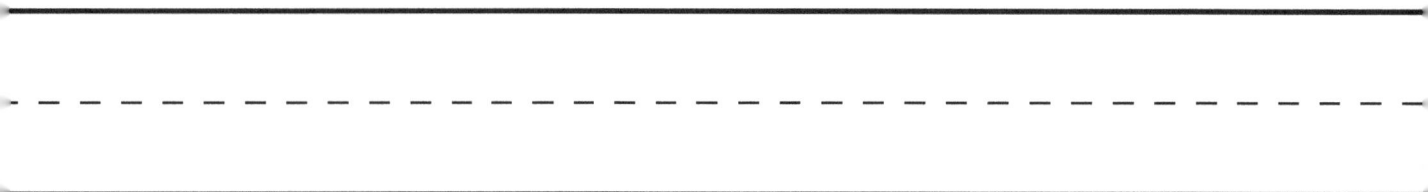

T t

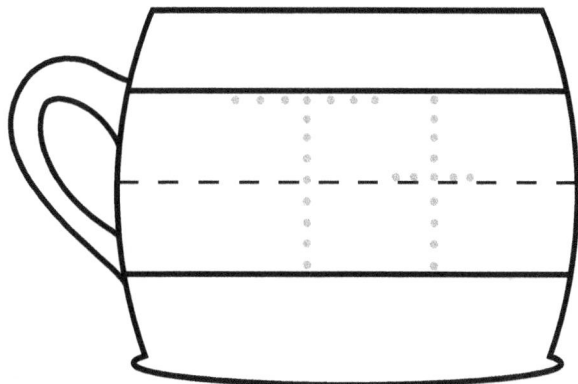

Uu

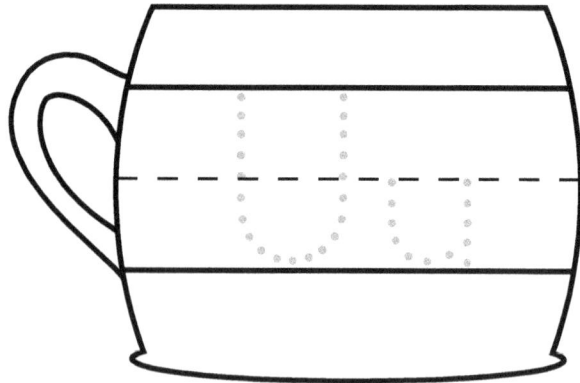

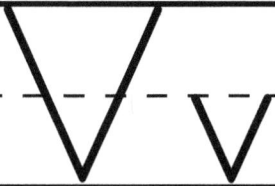

V v v v v v v v

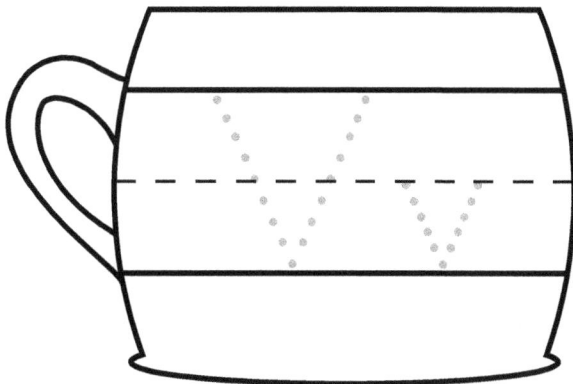

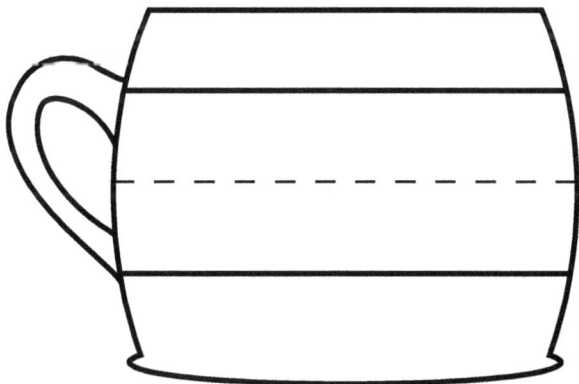

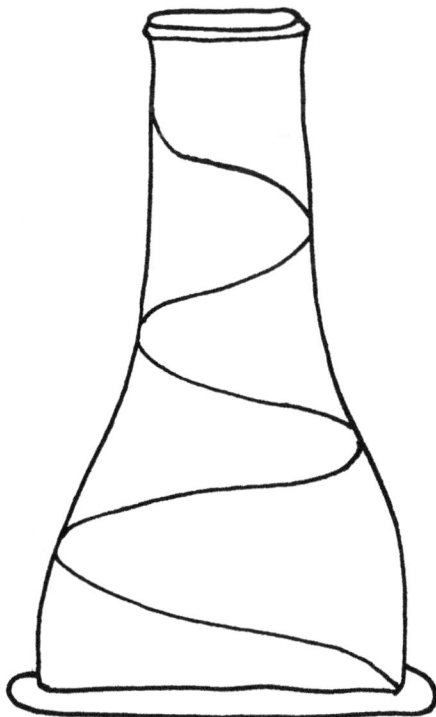

Ww

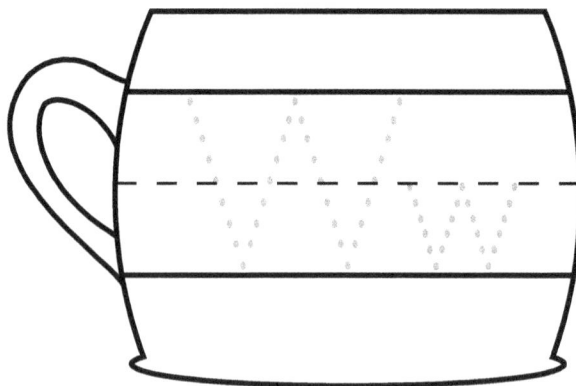

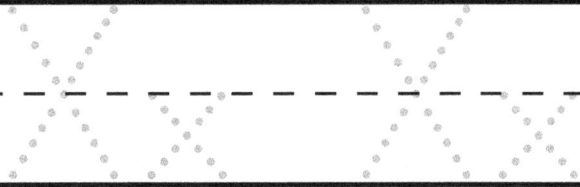

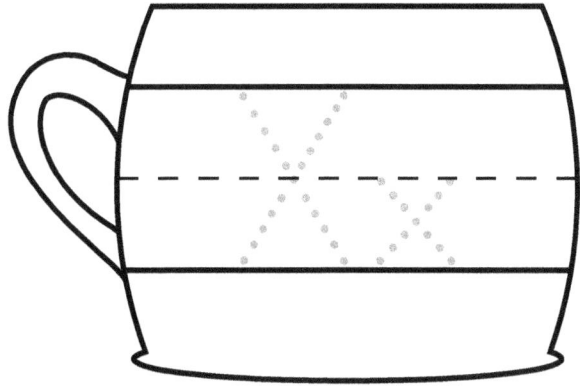

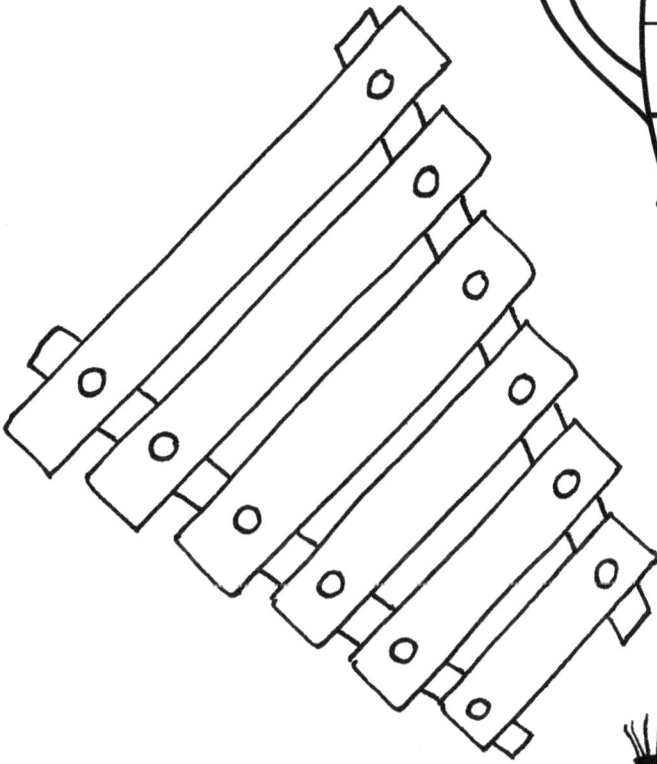

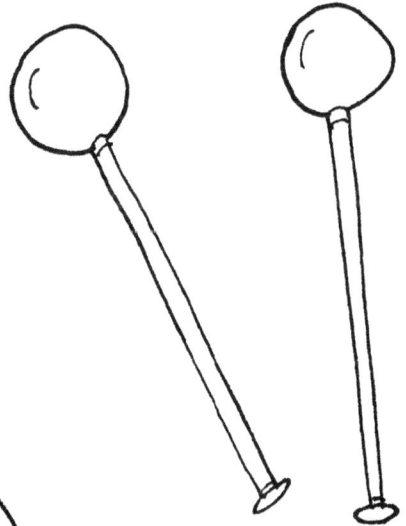

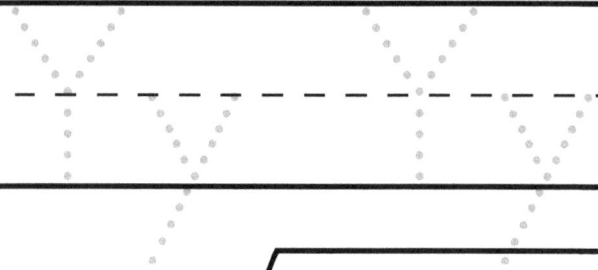
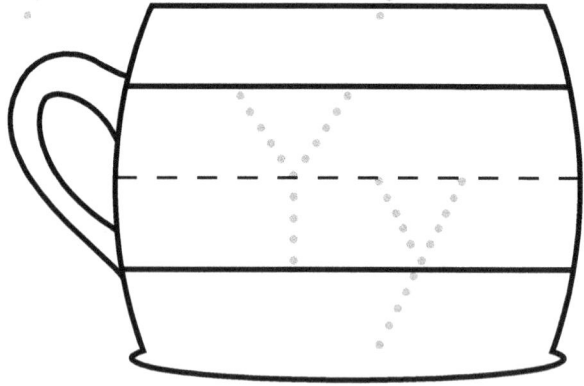
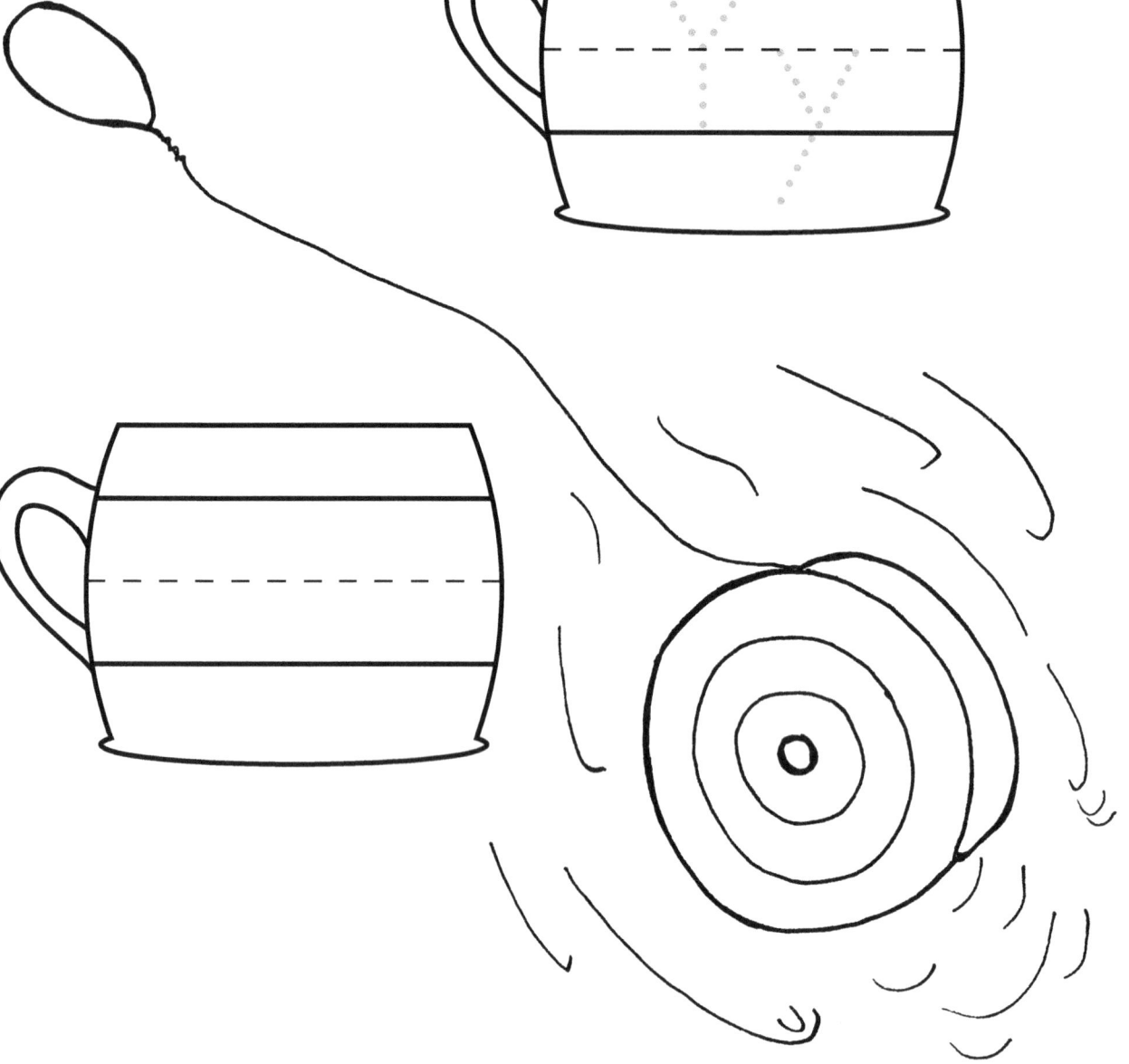
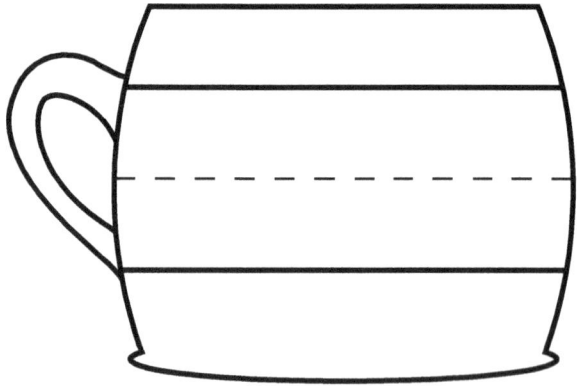
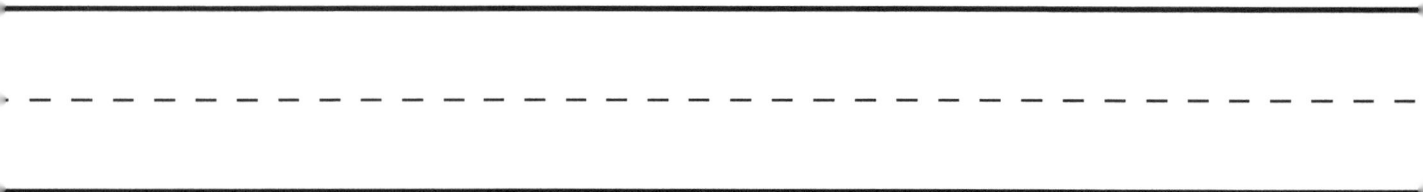

Zz

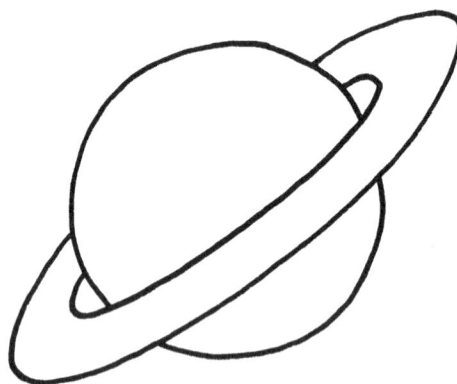

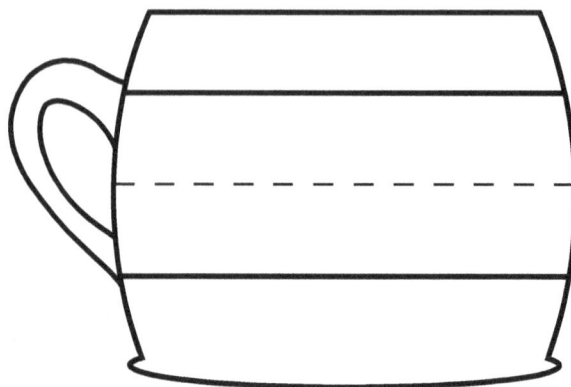

1 2 3 4 5 6 7 8 9 10

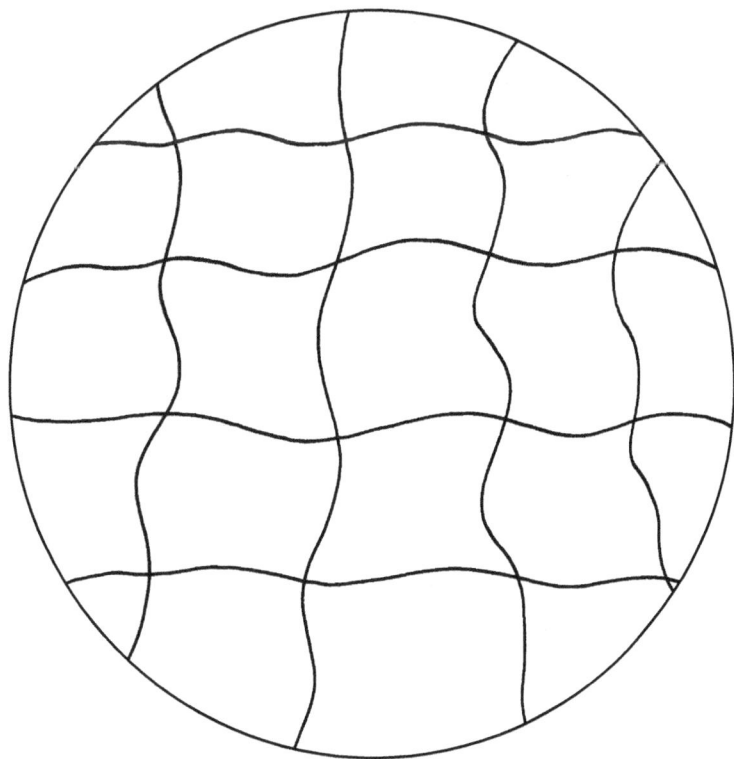

Practice Page

Practice Page

Practice Page

One

1   1

one

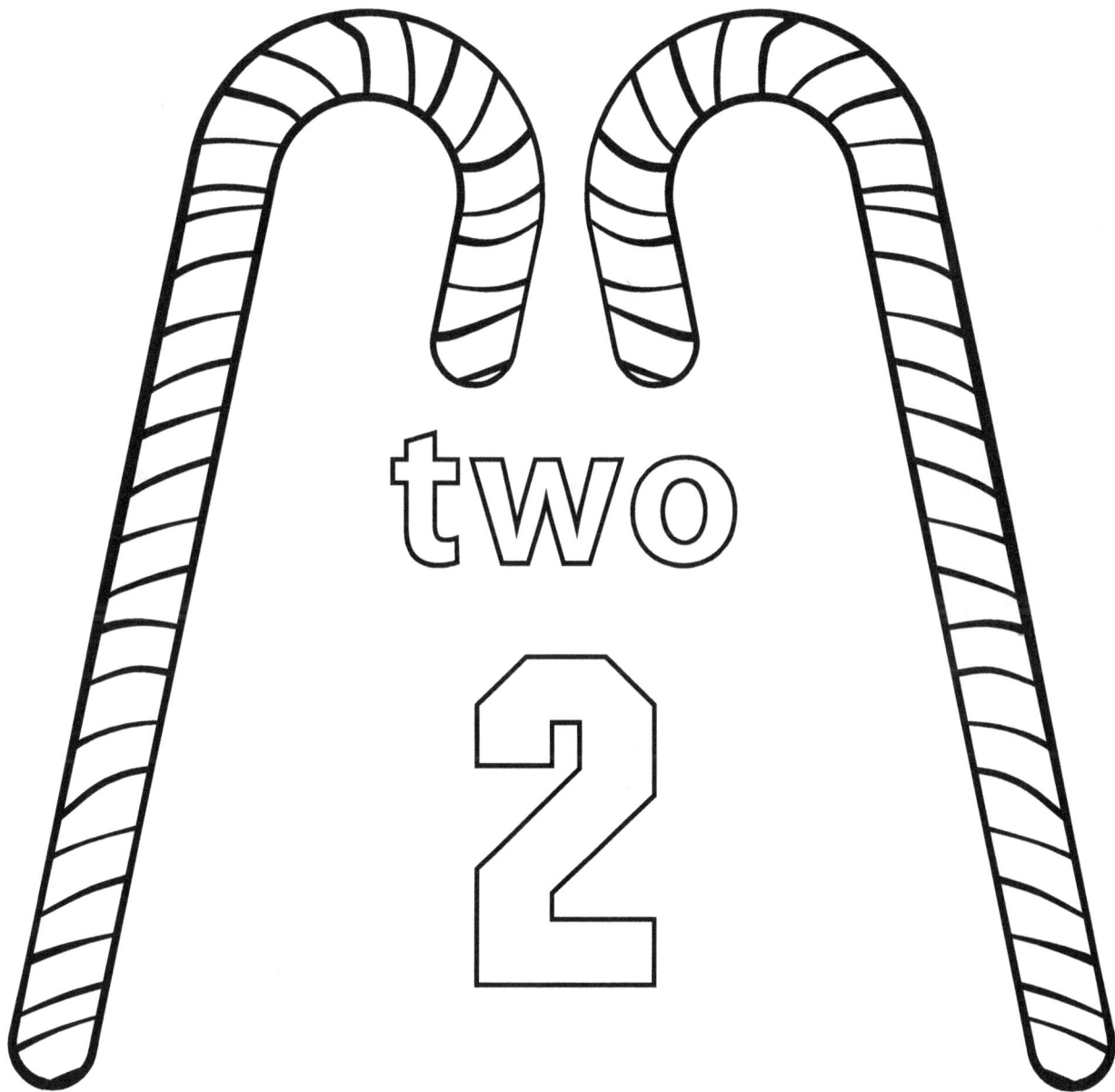

two

2

2 2 2

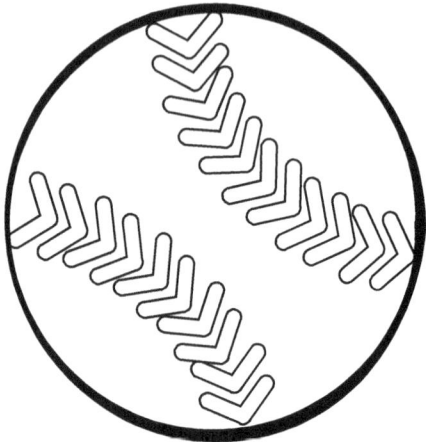
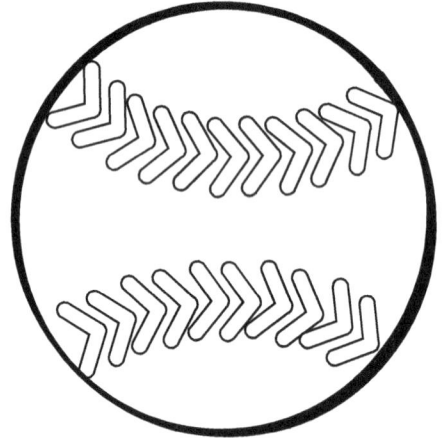

3

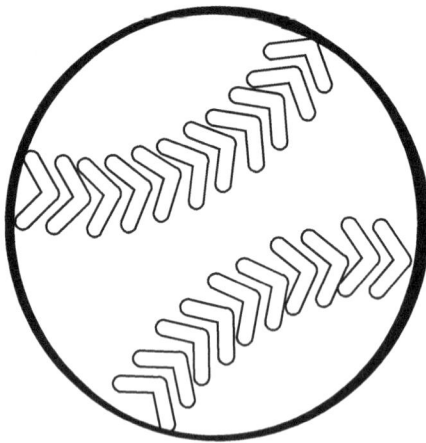

three

four

4

four

5

five

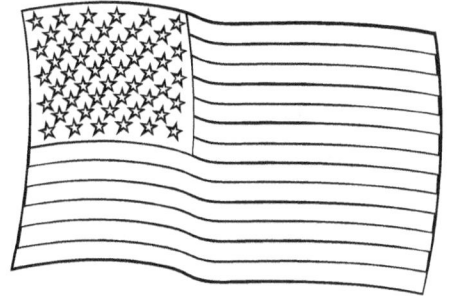

6

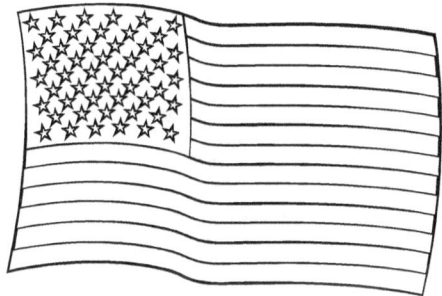

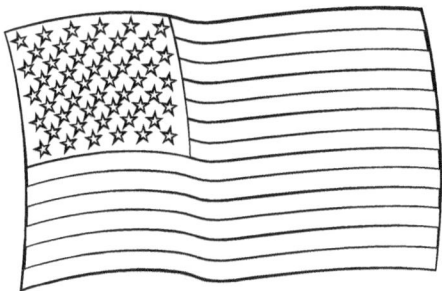
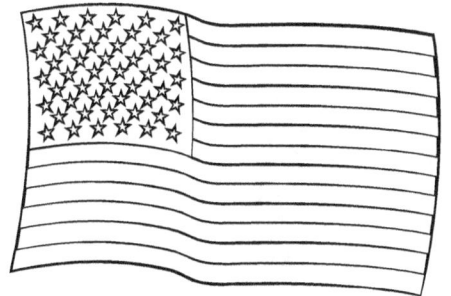

six

7

seven

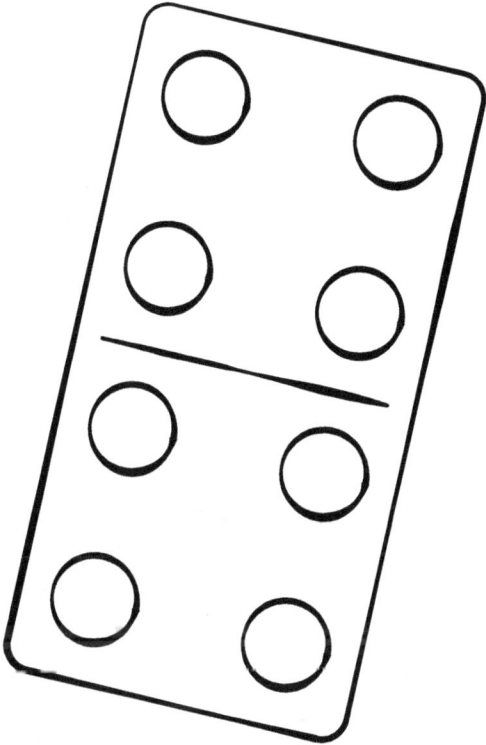
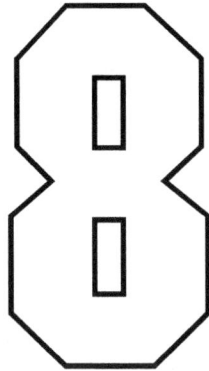
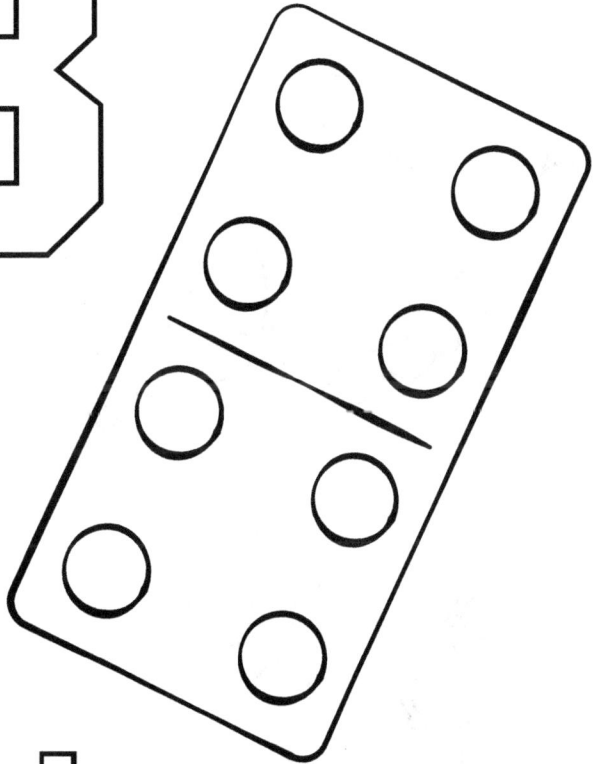

eight

Nine

9

nine

10
ten

11
eleven

twelve

 13

thirteen

14

fourteen

fifteen

16

sixteen

17

seventeen

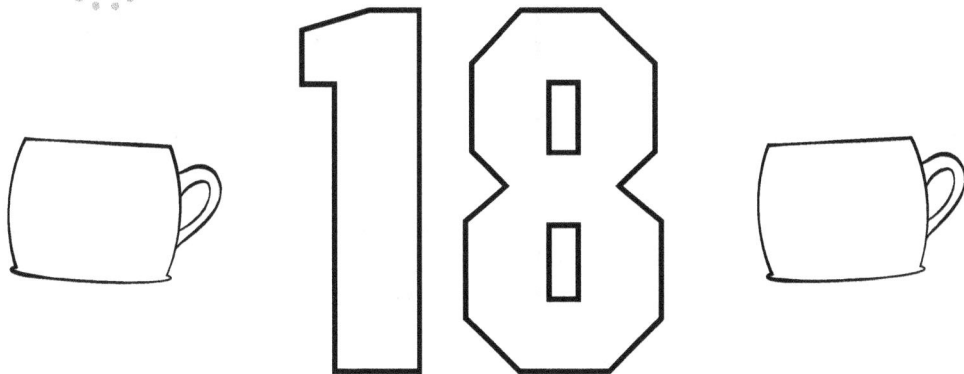

eighteen

  **19**

nineteen

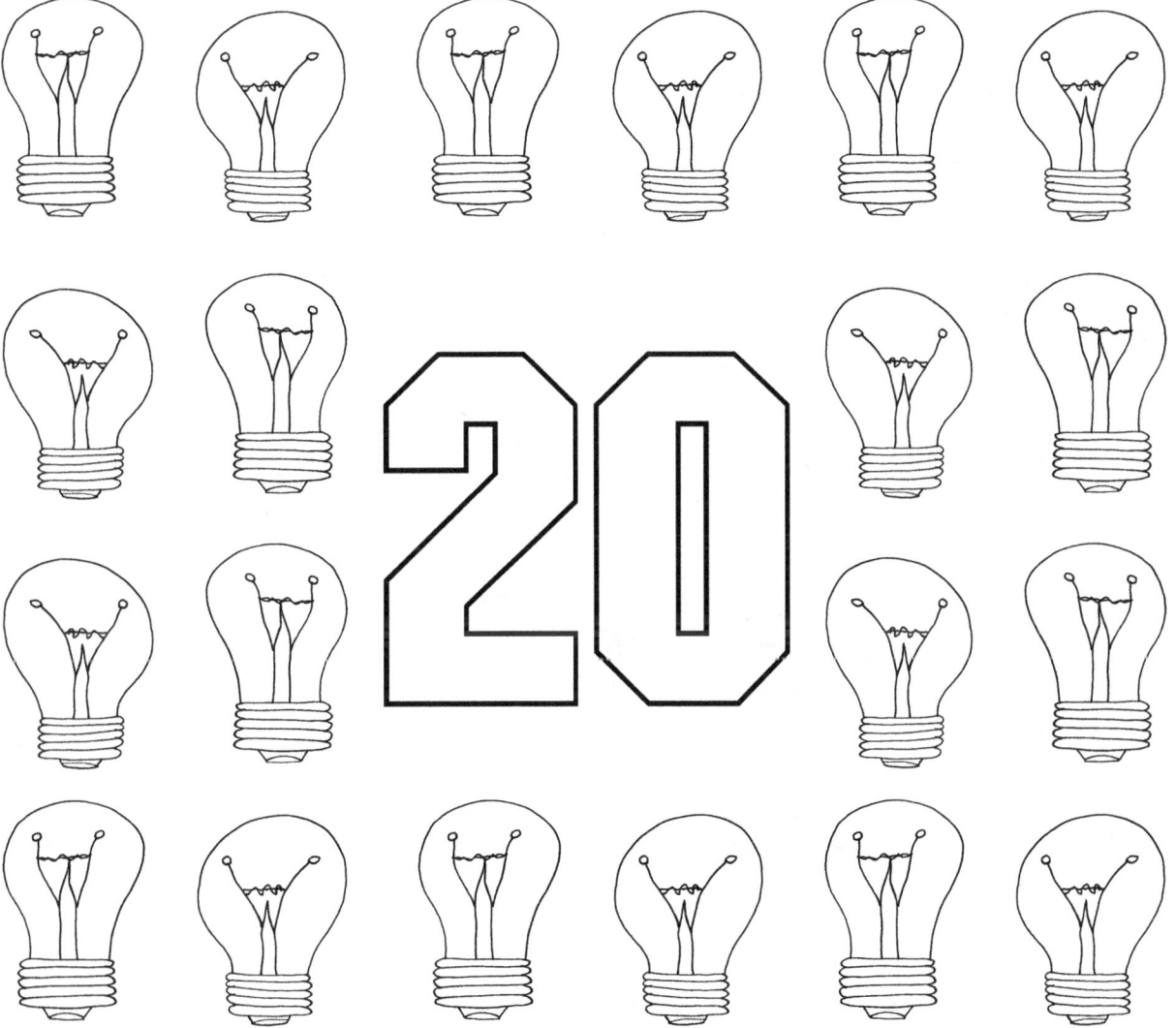

twenty

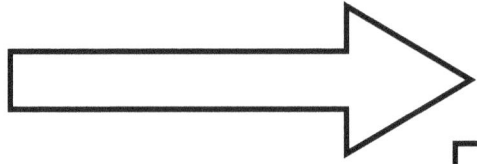

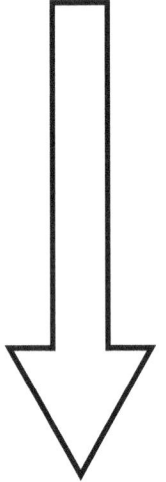

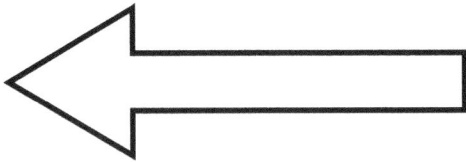

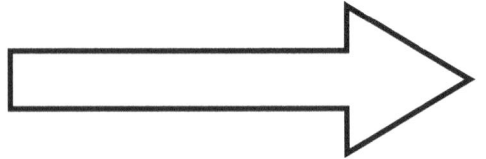

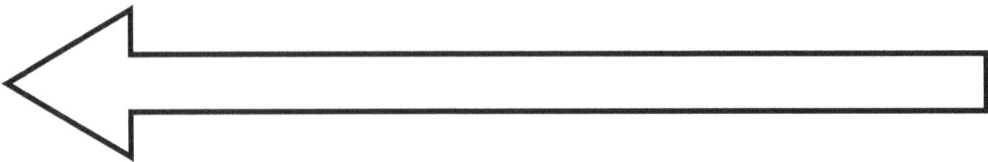

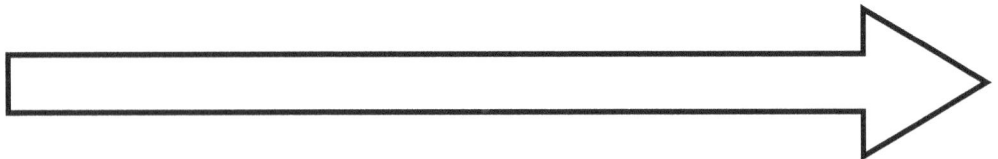

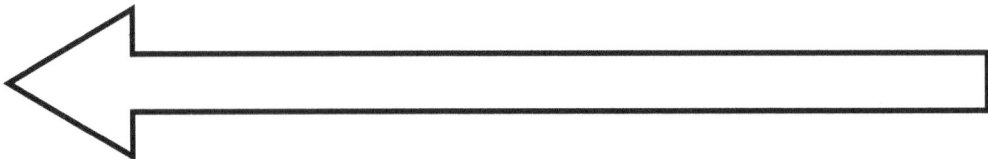

1	2 ABC	3 DEF
4 GHI	5 JKL	6 MNO
7 PQRS	8 TUV	9 WXYZ
*	0	#

Your phone # is: _____

Emergency phone # is: _____

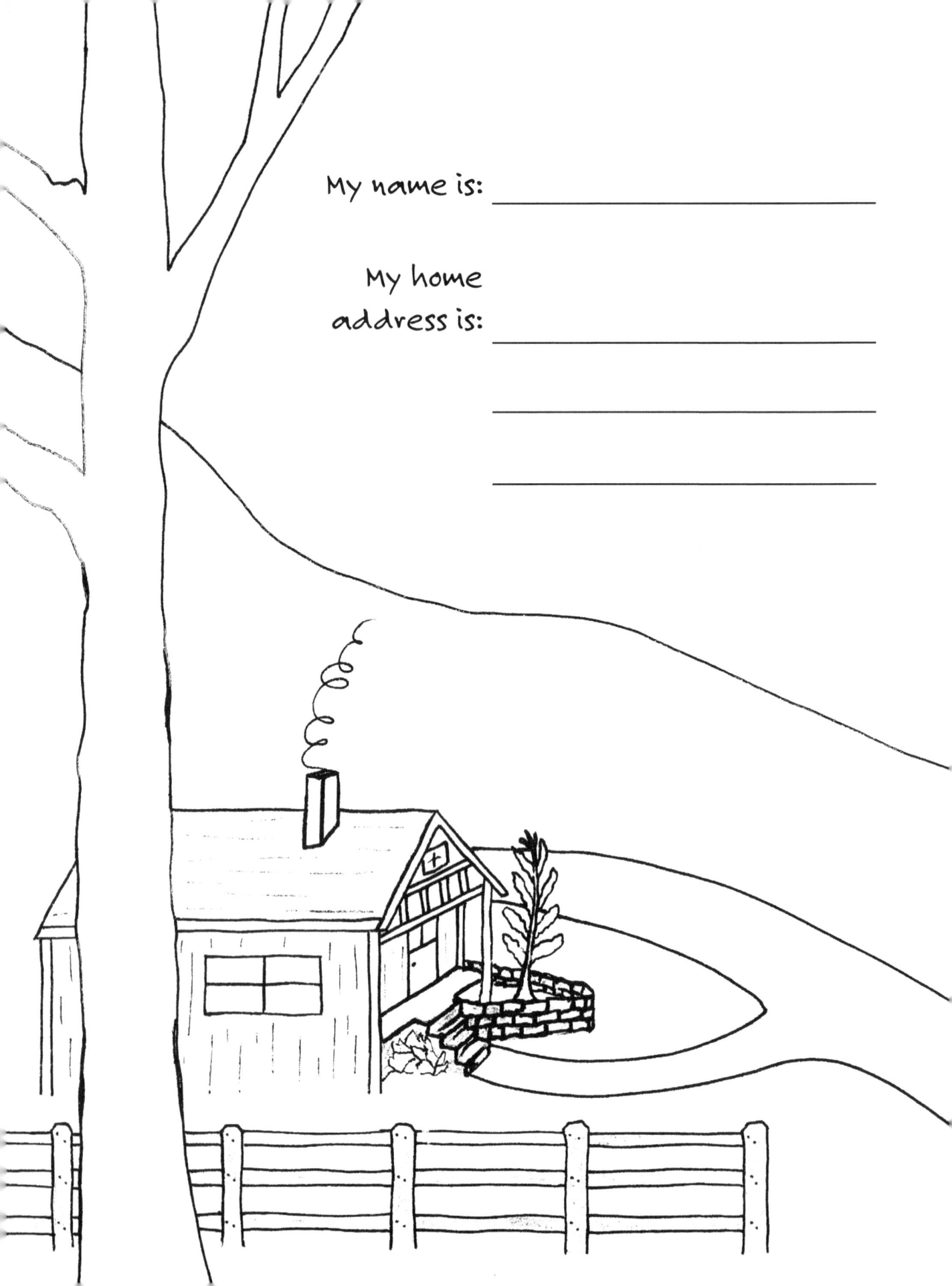

My name is: _____

My home
address is: _____

_____

_____

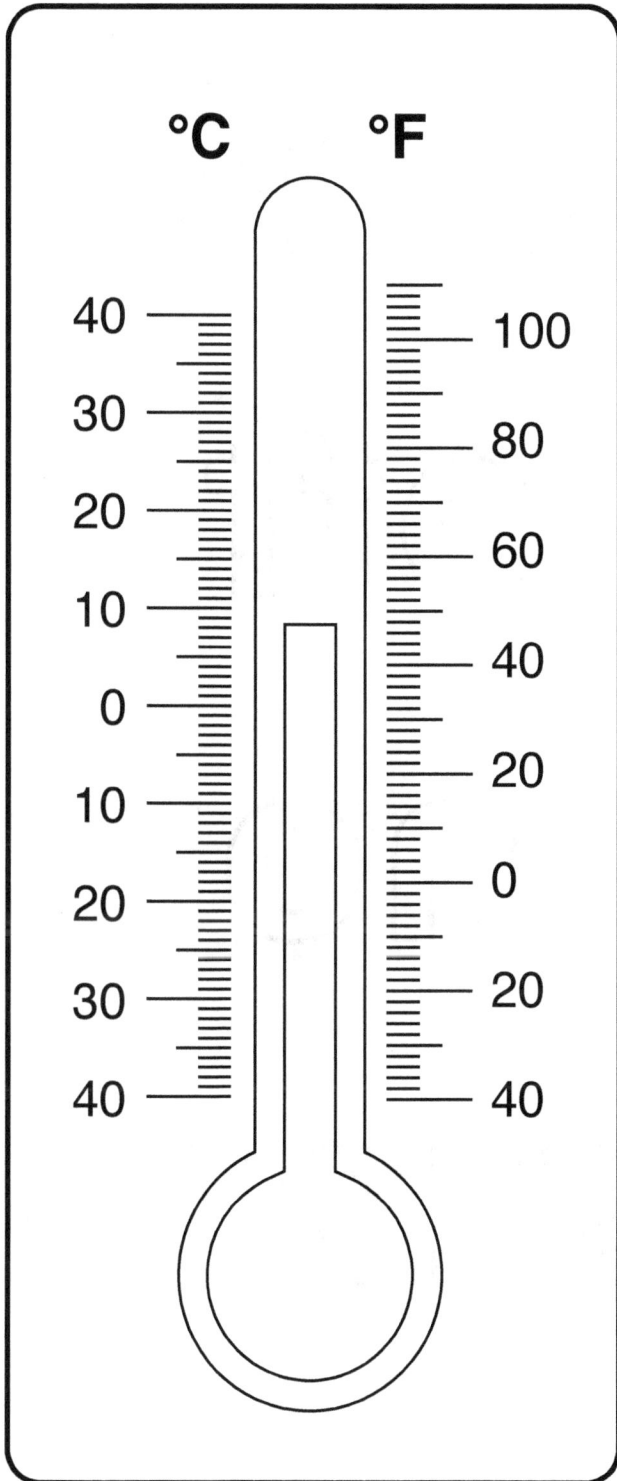

°C °F

40 — — 100
30 — — 80
20 — — 60
10 — — 40
0 — — 20
10 — — 0
20 — — 20
30 — — 40
40 — — 40

hot

cold

fire

ice

What is the temperature today?

_____

in out

on off

yes no

 stop

go

Teacup Trudy Loves Me®

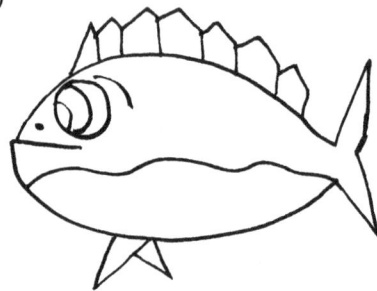

fish

what is your favorite time of day?

Practice Page

www.ingramcontent.com/pod-product-compliance
Lightning Source LLC
Chambersburg PA
CBHW081223020426
42331CB00012B/3079

* 9 7 8 0 6 9 2 7 8 9 9 2 6 *